MW00955572

Dysgraphia tools for kids

100 activities and games to improve writing skills in kids with dysgraphia and dyslexia

Volume 2

Kristy B. Rogers

Introduction

Teaching a child with dyslexia to read: Dyslexia is a specific and persistent learning disability that affects reading and writing. Teaching a child with dyslexia to read and write can become a difficult challenge for families and educators to tackle. For these children, written language becomes a great barrier, often without meaning or logic, which generates rejection of the task, frustration and discomfort.

A child with dyslexia has significant difficulties in these areas because their brain processes information differently than other children, which is why if we expect the same results following the traditional method, we will find many barriers that can and often do harm the child. It is important to become aware of the areas where the child struggles, to help them overcome these difficulties and make reading an easier task.

Reading difficulties with dyslexia

Dyslexia is a neurobiological disorder that affects the development and structuring of certain areas of the brain. Therefore, it causes the brain to process information differently, making it difficult for the person to understand letters, their sounds, their combinations, etc.

Human language is a language based on signs, letters and their sounds, which are arbitrary. The relationship between each grapheme (letter) with its phoneme (sound), does not follow any logic; it's simply chance. This is one of the greatest difficulties that children face when they have to learn to read and write. Converting spoken language into signs and symbols, and transforming sounds into letters, is a challenge. This is even more complicated in children with dyslexia; the relationship becomes something indecipherable for them. No matter how hard they try, they cannot make sense of that dance between letters and sounds.

Children with dyslexia have trouble recognizing letters, sometimes they mistake letters for others, write them backwards, etc. They also have a hard time knowing the sound that corresponds to each letter; and things get even more complicated when we combine several letters and we have to know several sounds. Learning new words is also a challenge and they can easily forget them, so it's important that the child works hard to acquire them. Sometimes they read certain words effortlessly, but the next day they completely forget them. When they write, they omit letters, change their position, forget words in a sentence, etc.

Dyslexia also affects reading comprehension. When reading, they are trying really hard to decipher and understand each word, sometimes even each letter; that is why the meaning of the text gets lost.

Activities to help develop reading comprehension in children

How to teach a child with dyslexia to read:

A child with dyslexia has difficulty learning to read and write, because it is hard for them to recognize letters and know which sound, they correspond to. However, the child can learn to overcome those difficulties. Remember that dyslexia is a learning difficulty that does not imply any physical or mental handicap; the child with dyslexia has adequate capacities. In order to teach a child with dyslexia to read, it is essential to know the nature of their difficulties, understand them and use a teaching method that responds to their needs.

A teaching method to help the child read:

In the first place, it is necessary to assess the child's reading and writing level and the nature and characteristics of their difficulties, so as to understand their specific needs. For this, it's advisable to seek a specialist. Reading favors the development of phonological awareness (which consists of the letter-sound correspondence). To do this, start with simple activities, letter by letter, even if other children around the same age read full texts. Later, we can continue with full words, phrases and texts. It is about dedicating more time and more detail to the learning process.

Phonological awareness worksheets

Use motivational activities that are engaging. Do not limit the child to just paper and pencil: they can make letters out of play dough, write on sand with their fingers, play catch or games such as hangman, word searches, crossword puzzles, etc. Don't force them to read or read a lot. Try to have them read on a daily basis, little by little; sometimes a sentence or a paragraph is enough. Help them understand what they read, ask them questions, ask them to read again, etc.

Copyright 2022 - All Rights Reserved

Contents of this book may not be reproduced, duplicated or transmitted without direct written permission from the author. Under no circumstances will any legal responsibility or blame be held against the publisher for any reparation, damages or monetary loss due to information herein, either directly or indirectly.

Legal Notice:

You cannot amend, distribute, sell, use, quote or paraphrase any part of the contents within this book without the consent of the author.

Disclaimer note:

Please note that the information contained within this document serves only for educational and entertainment purposes. No warranties of any kind are expressed or implied. Readers acknowledge that the author is not engaging in the rendering of legal, financial, medical or professional advice.

TABLE OF CONTENTS

Trace the lines.

Trace the lines.

Trace the lines.

Trace the lines.

Trace the lines.

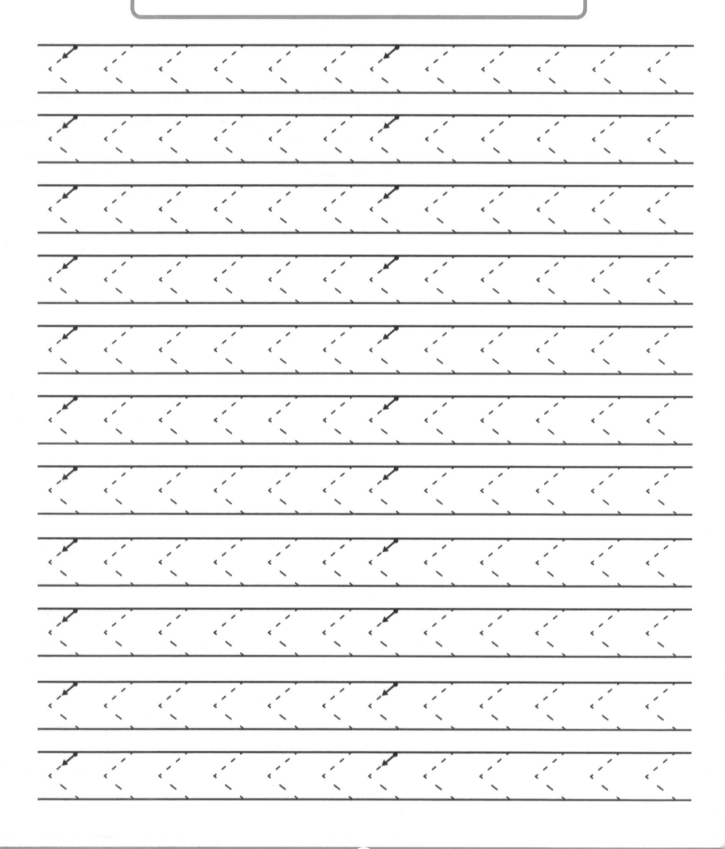

Trace the lines.

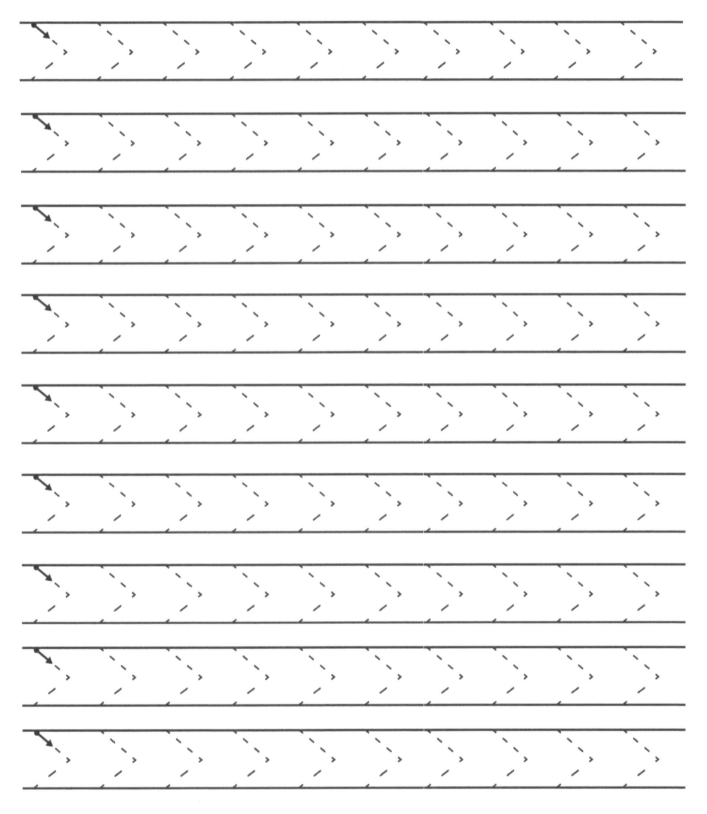

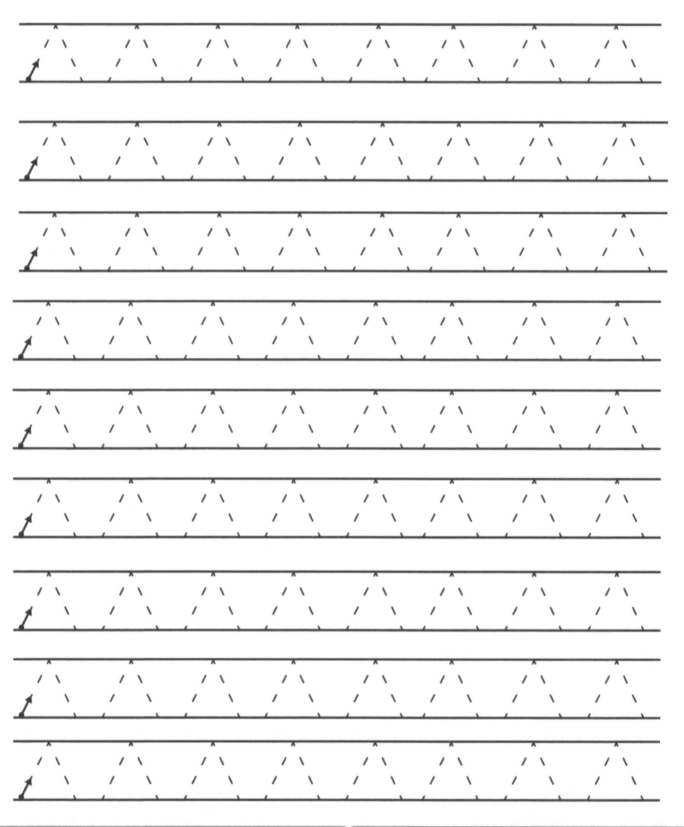

Trace the lines.

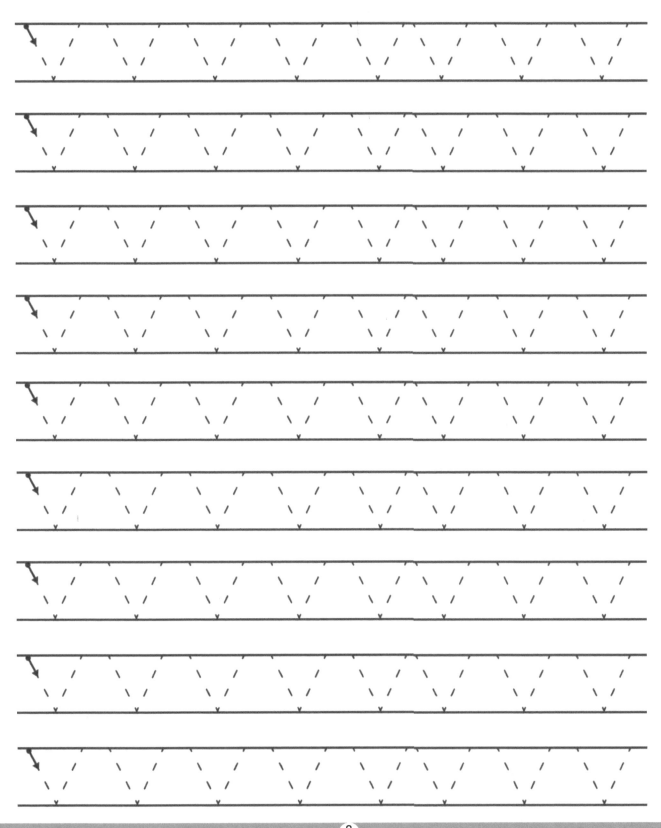

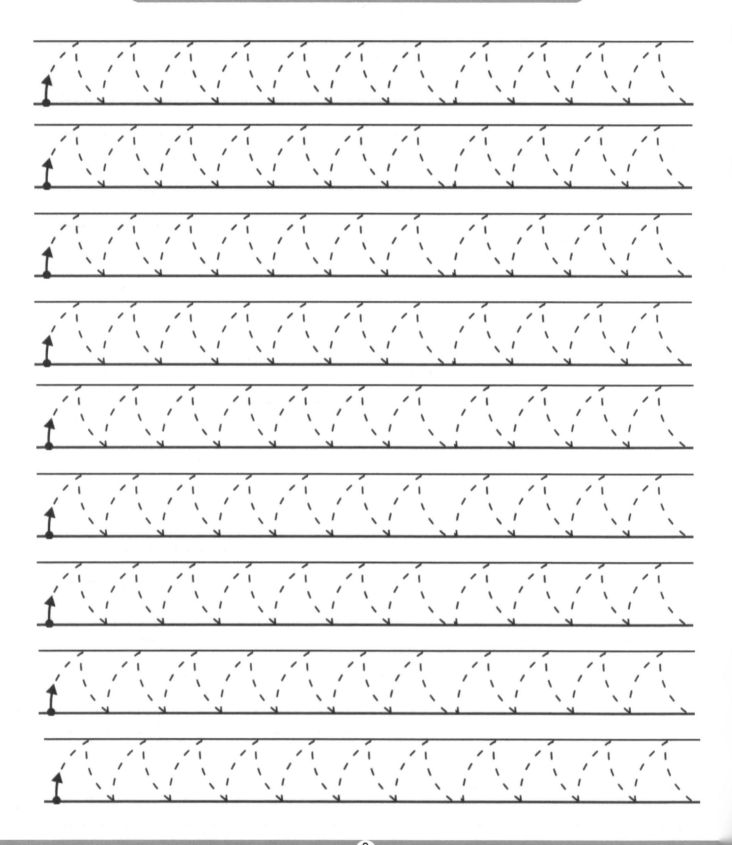

Trace the lines.

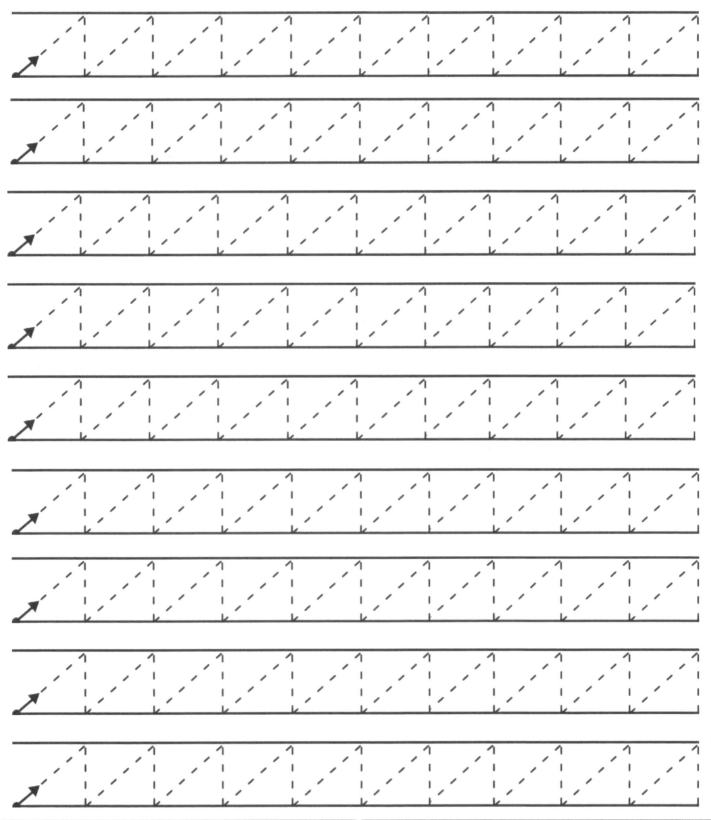

Trace the lines.

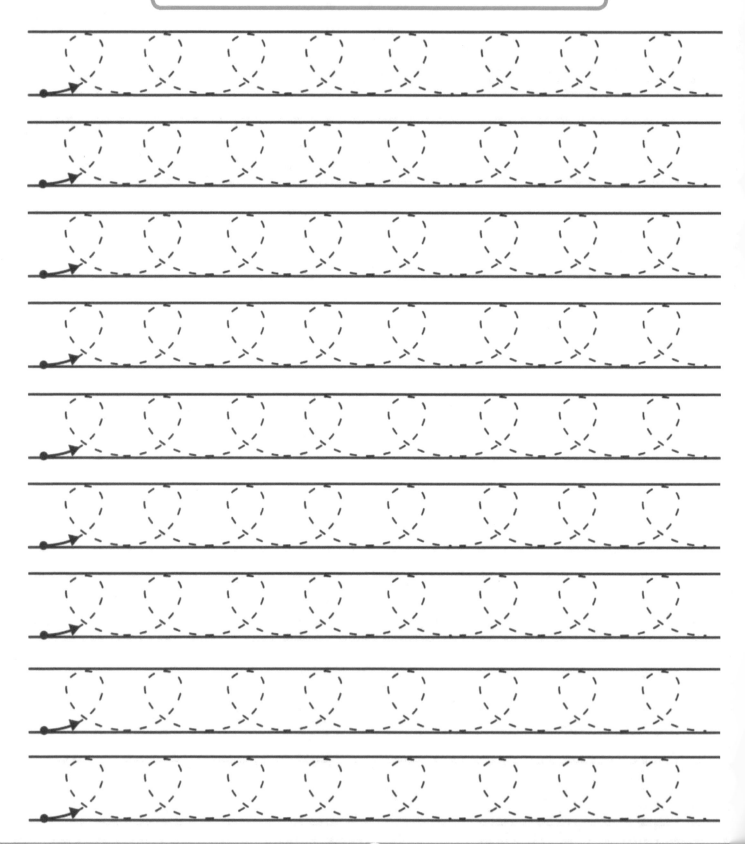

Trace the lines.

Trace the lines.

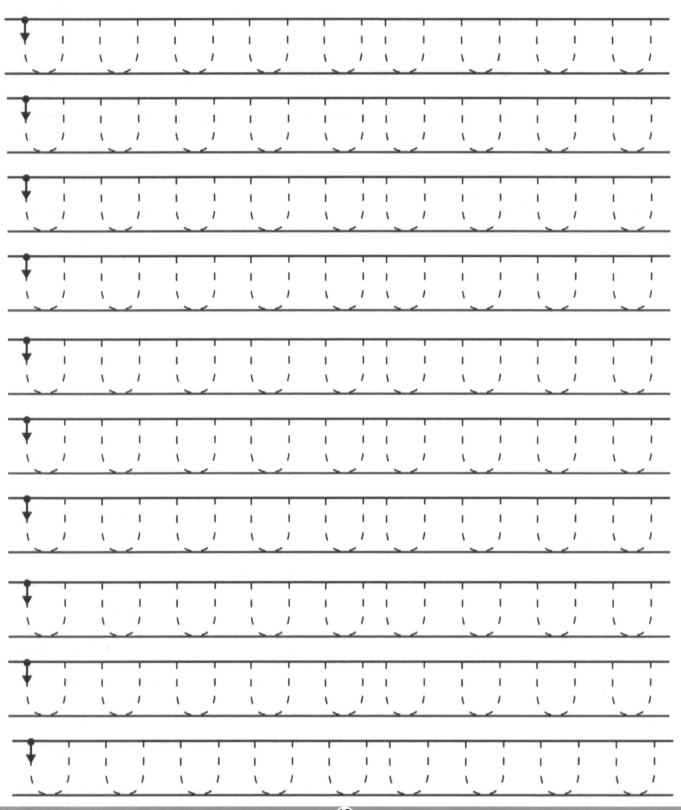

Trace the lines.

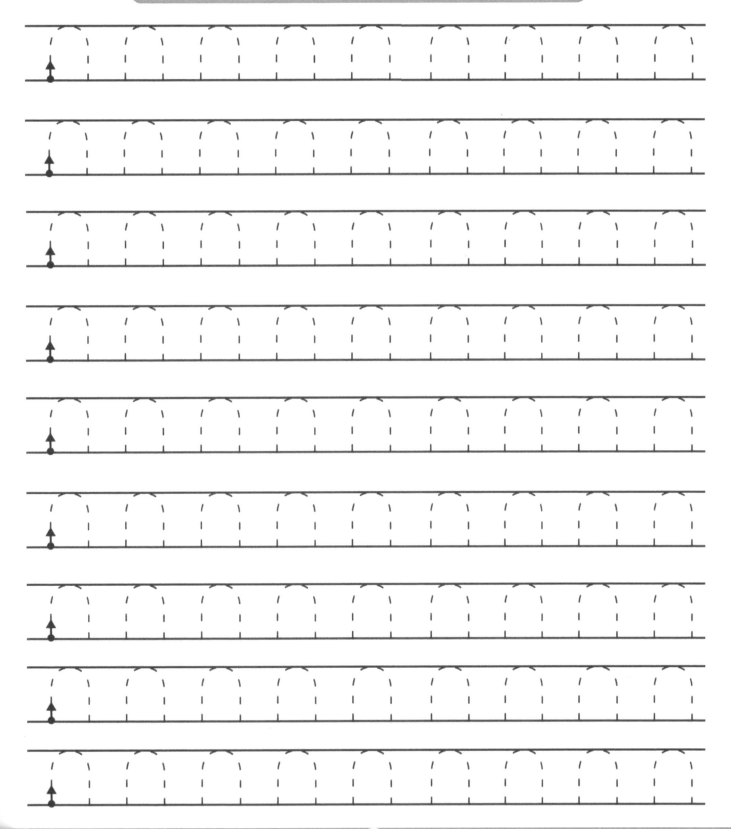

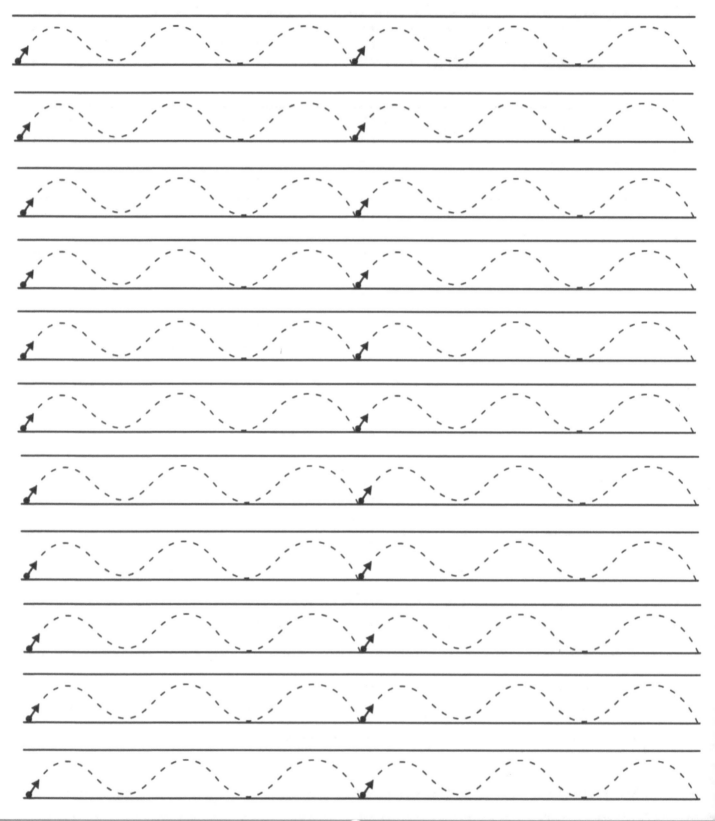

Trace the lines.

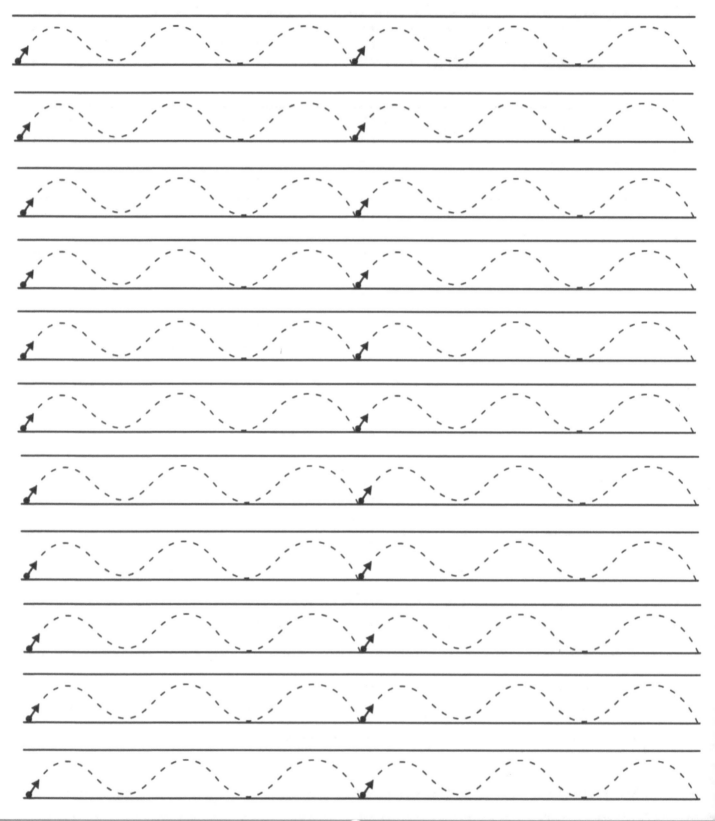

Trace the lines.

Trace the lines.

Trace the lines.

Trace the lines.

Trace the lines.

Draw the same bold line pattern in the boxes on the right.

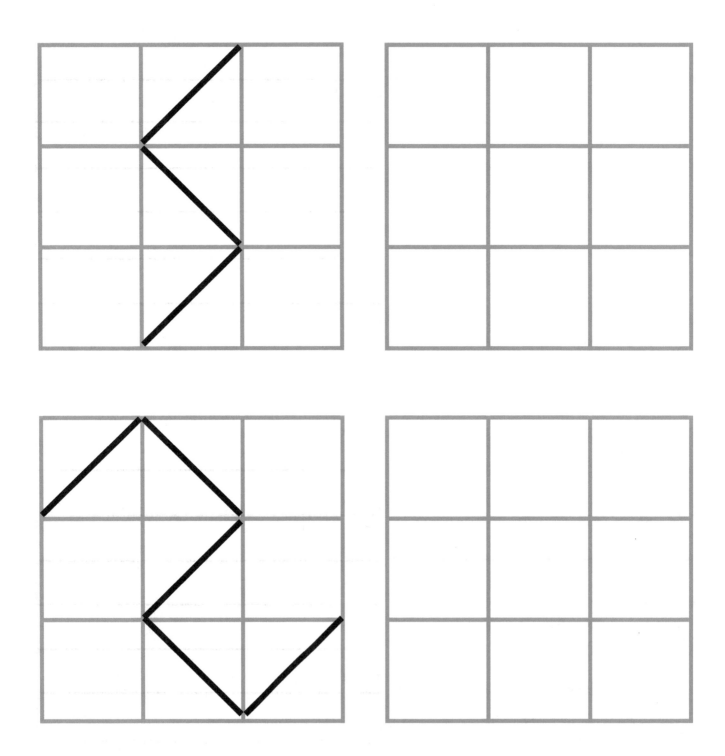

Draw the same bold line pattern in the boxes on the right.

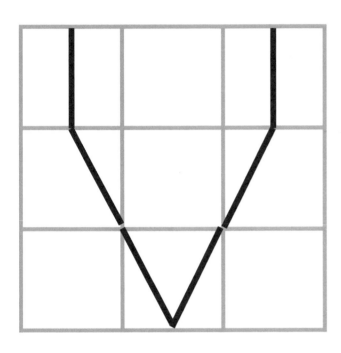
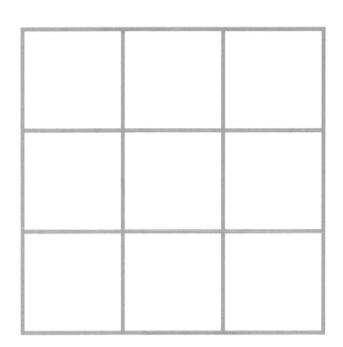

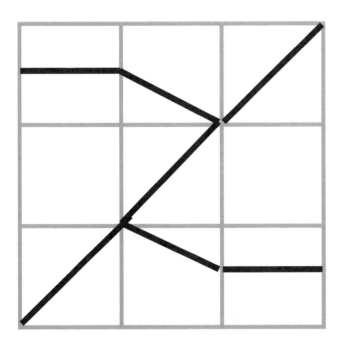
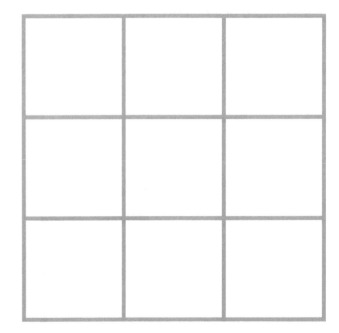

Draw the same bold line pattern in the boxes on the right.

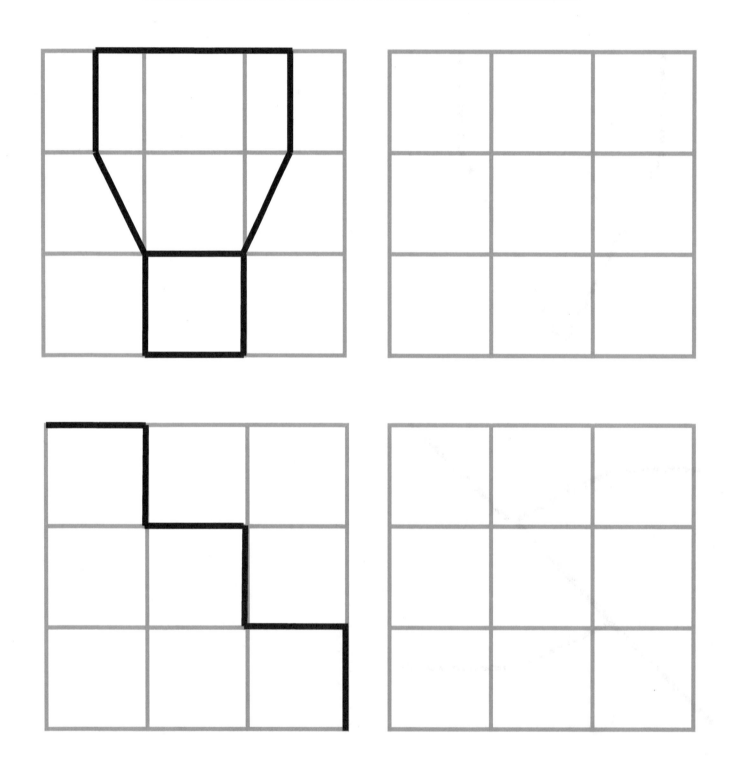

Draw the same bold line pattern in the boxes on the right.

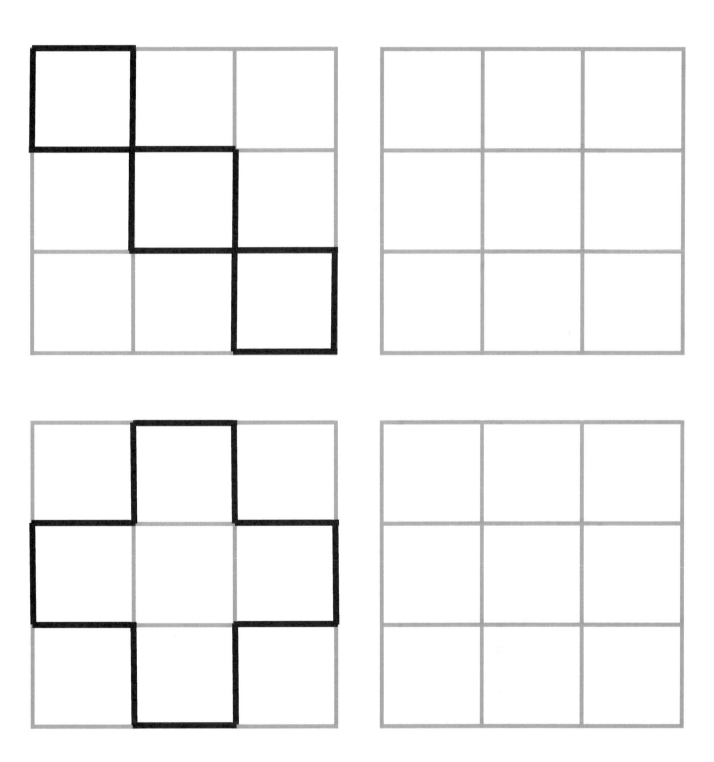

Draw the same bold line pattern in the boxes on the right.

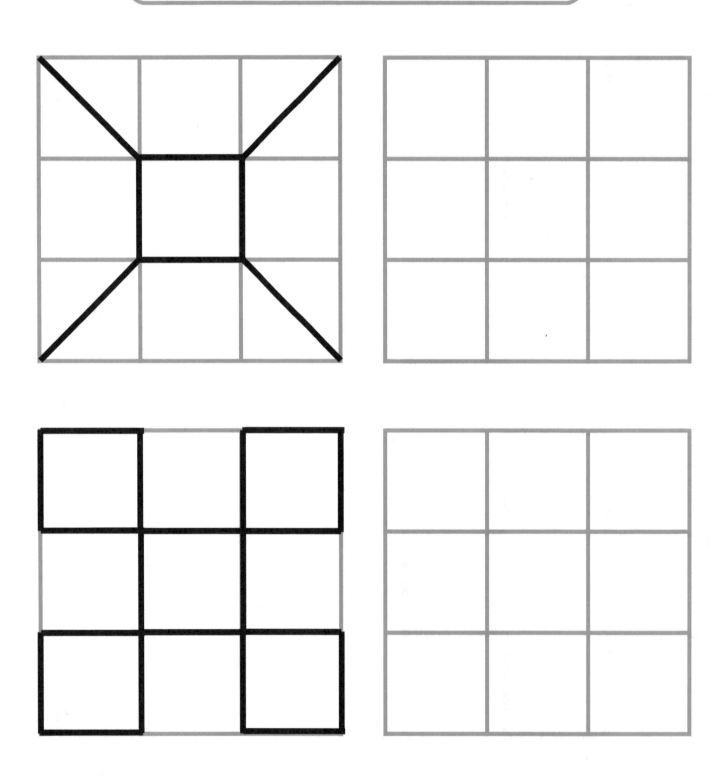

Draw the same bold line pattern in the boxes on the right.

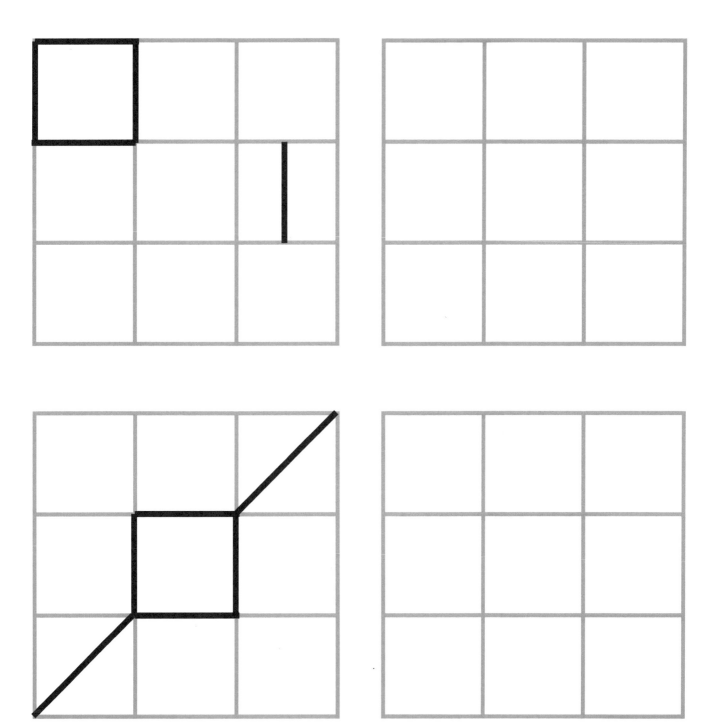

Draw the same bold line pattern in the boxes on the right.

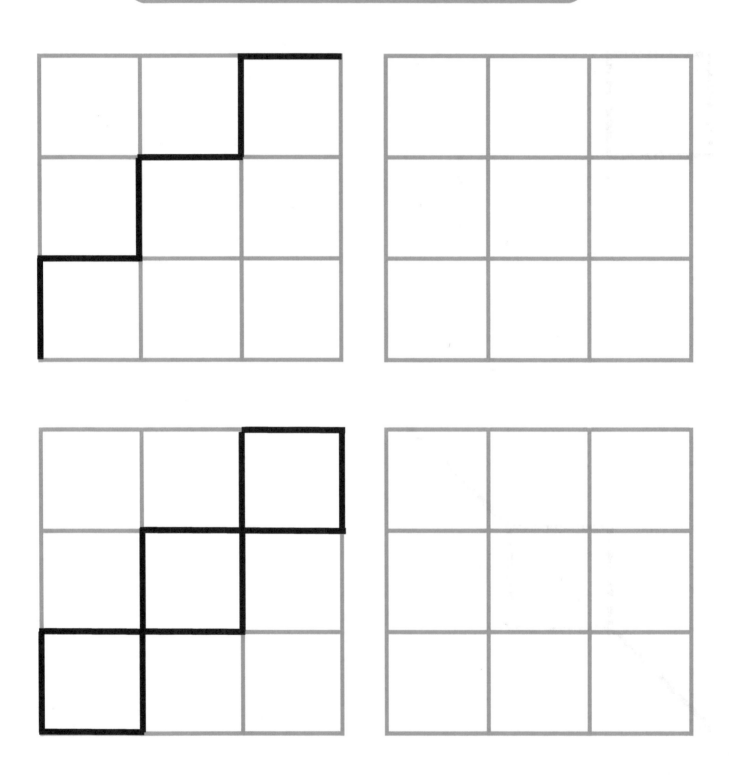

Draw the same bold line pattern in the boxes on the right.

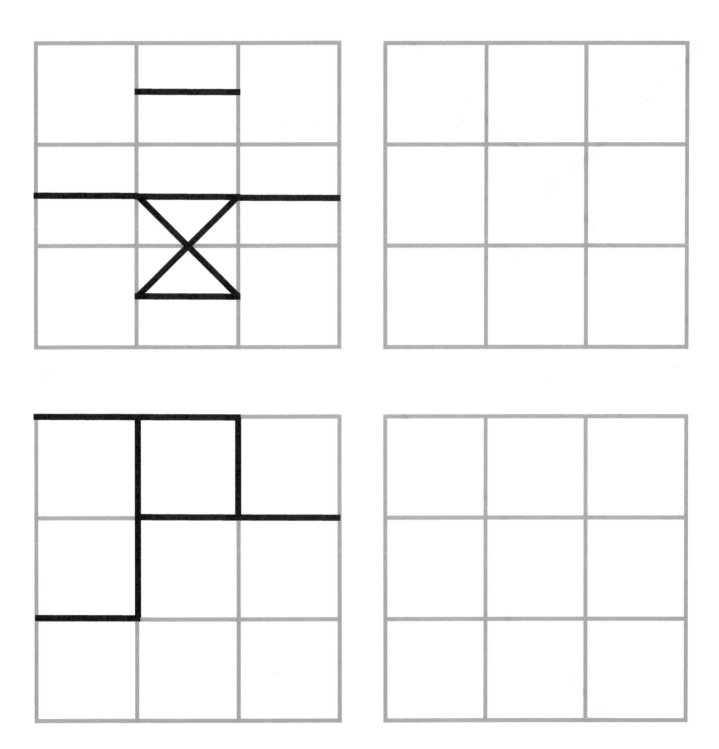

Draw the same bold line pattern in the boxes on the right.

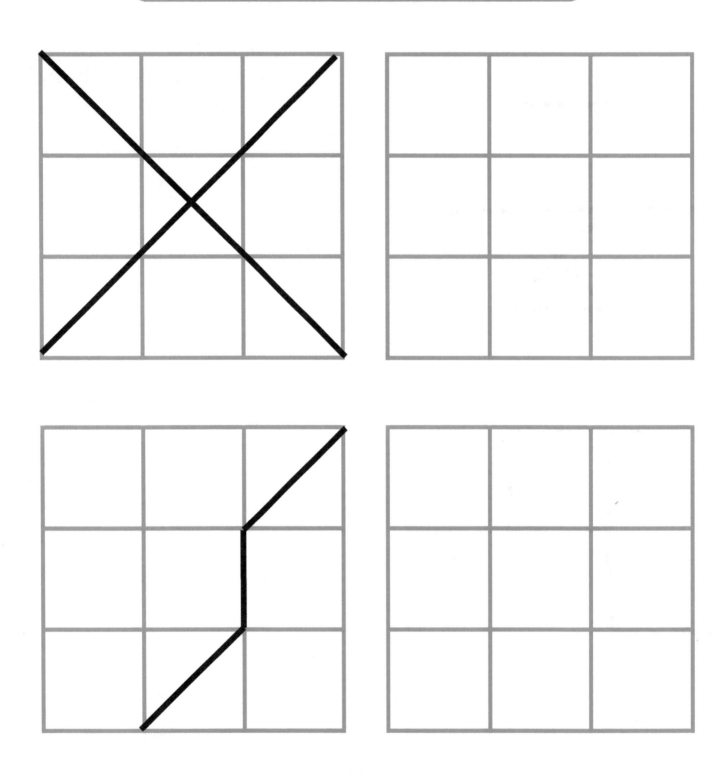

Draw the same bold line pattern in the boxes on the right.

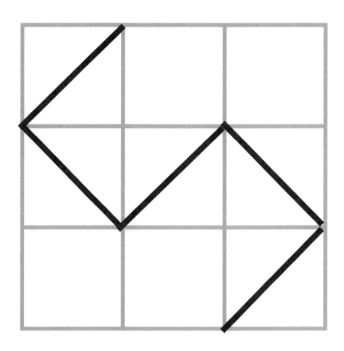
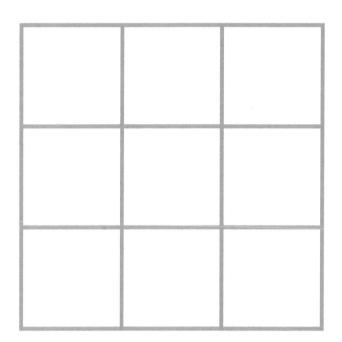

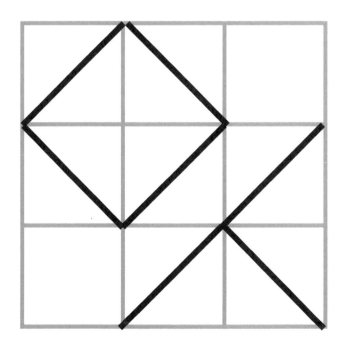
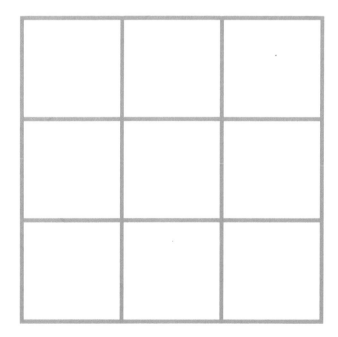

Look carefully at the left side of the drawing.
Make it symmetrical by drawing its
reflection on the right side of the dotted line.

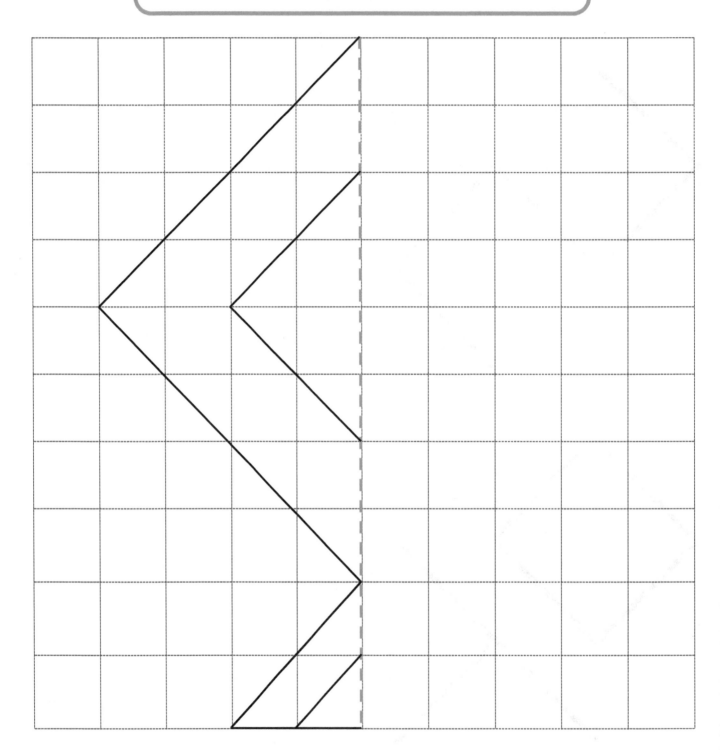

Look carefully at the left side of the drawing.
Make it symmetrical by drawing its
reflection on the right side of the dotted line.

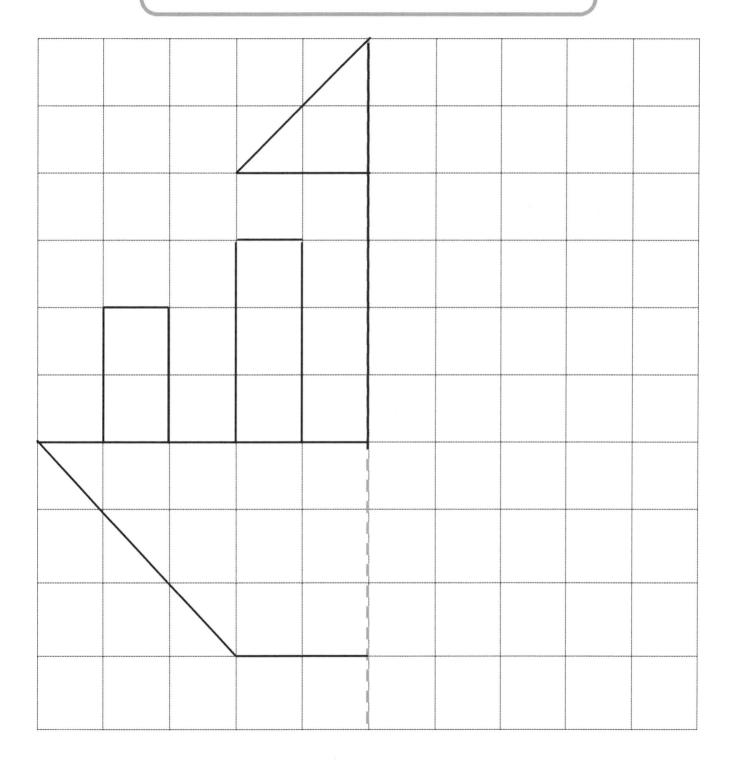

Look carefully at the left side of the drawing.
Make it symmetrical by drawing its
reflection on the right side of the dotted line.

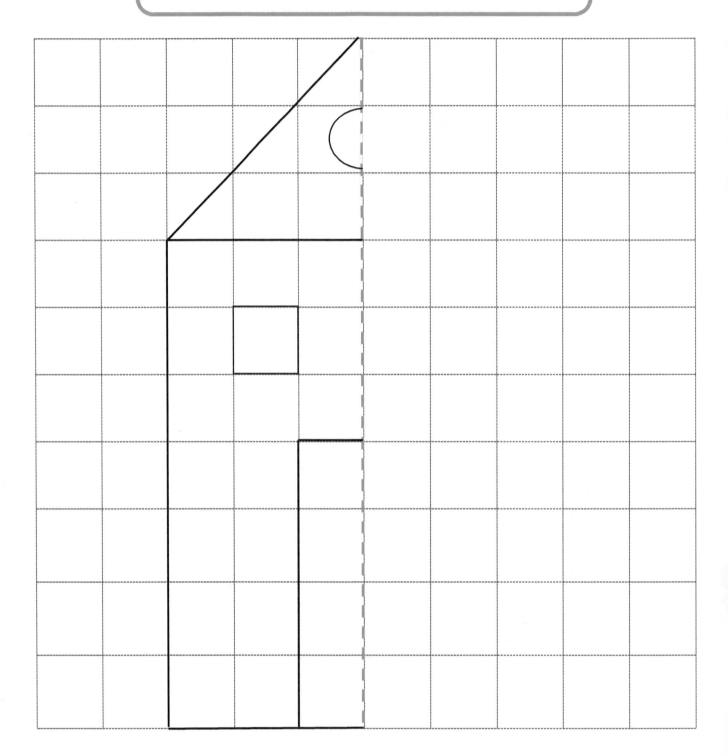

Look carefully at the left side of the drawing.
Make it symmetrical by drawing its
reflection on the right side of the dotted line.

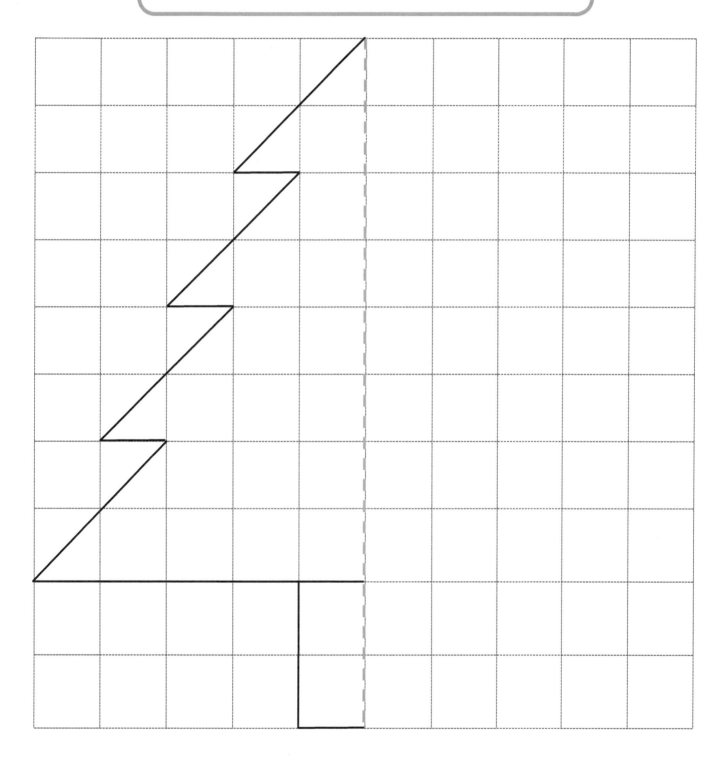

Look carefully at the left side of the drawing.
Make it symmetrical by drawing its
reflection on the right side of the dotted line.

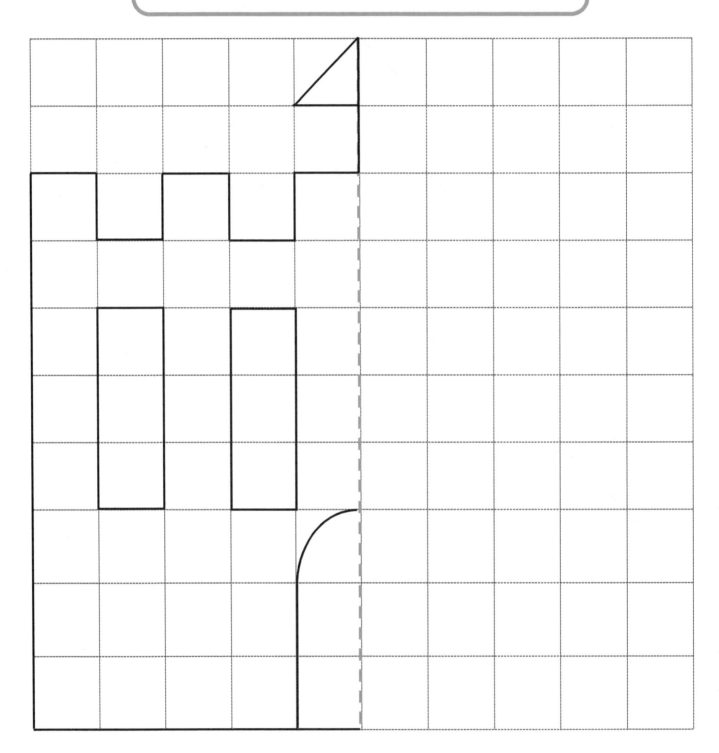

Look carefully at the left side of the drawing.
Make it symmetrical by drawing its
reflection on the right side of the dotted line.

Look carefully at the left side of the drawing.
Make it symmetrical by drawing its
reflection on the right side of the dotted line.

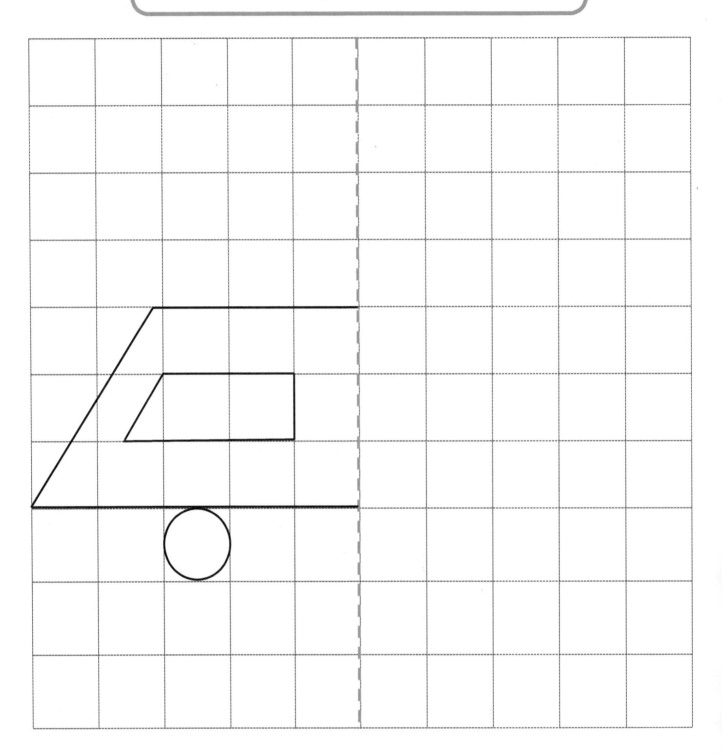

Look carefully at the left side of the drawing.
Make it symmetrical by drawing its
reflection on the right side of the dotted line.

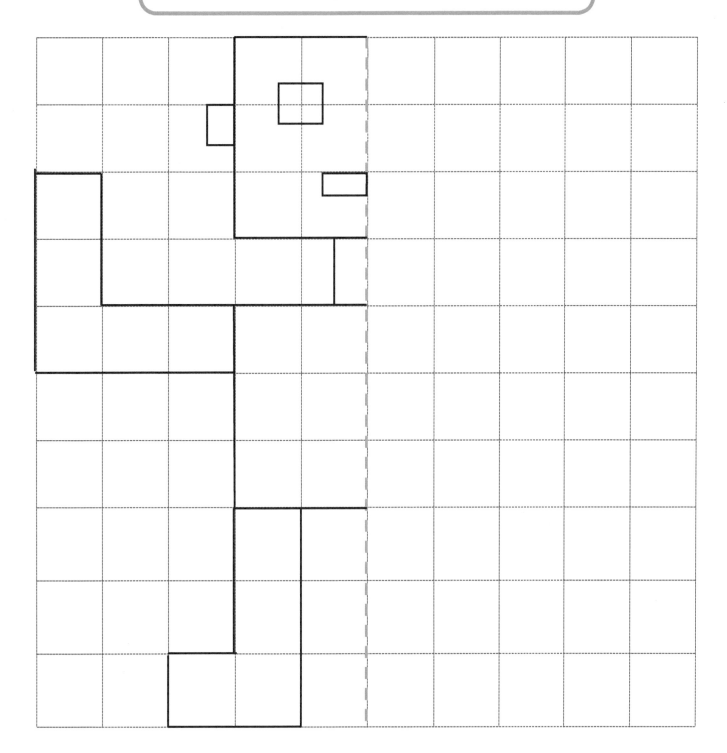

Look carefully at the left side of the drawing.
Make it symmetrical by drawing its
reflection on the right side of the dotted line.

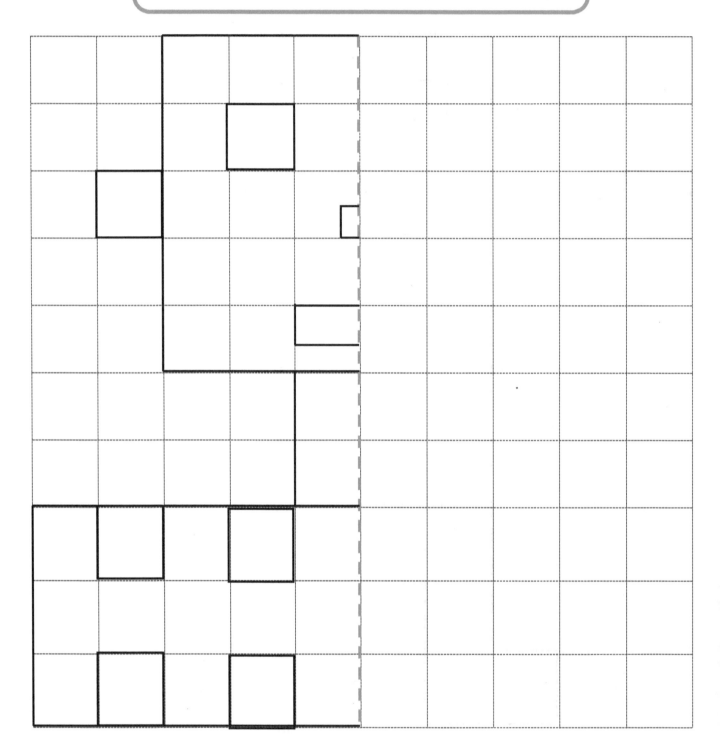

Look carefully at the left side of the drawing.
Make it symmetrical by drawing its
reflection on the right side of the dotted line.

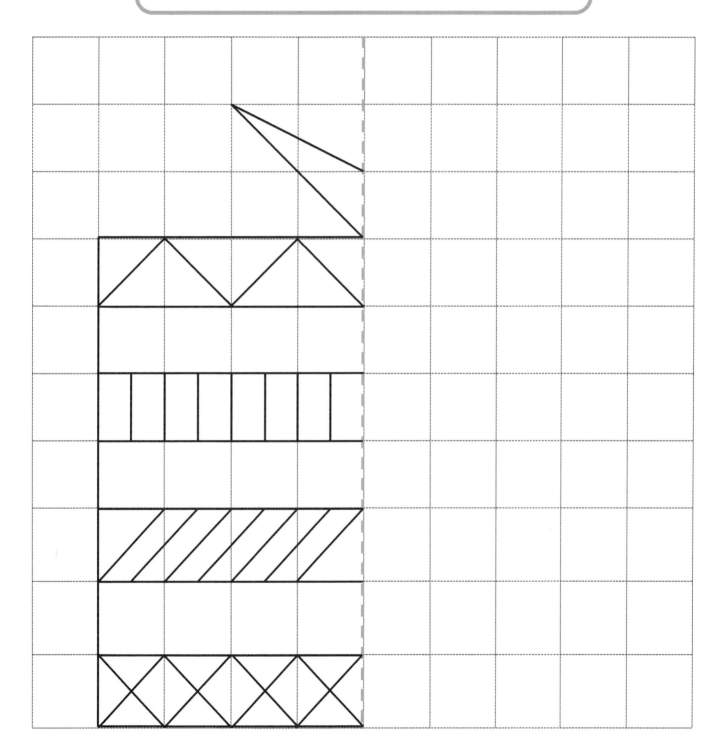

Copy the pattern from the top circle on the circle below it.

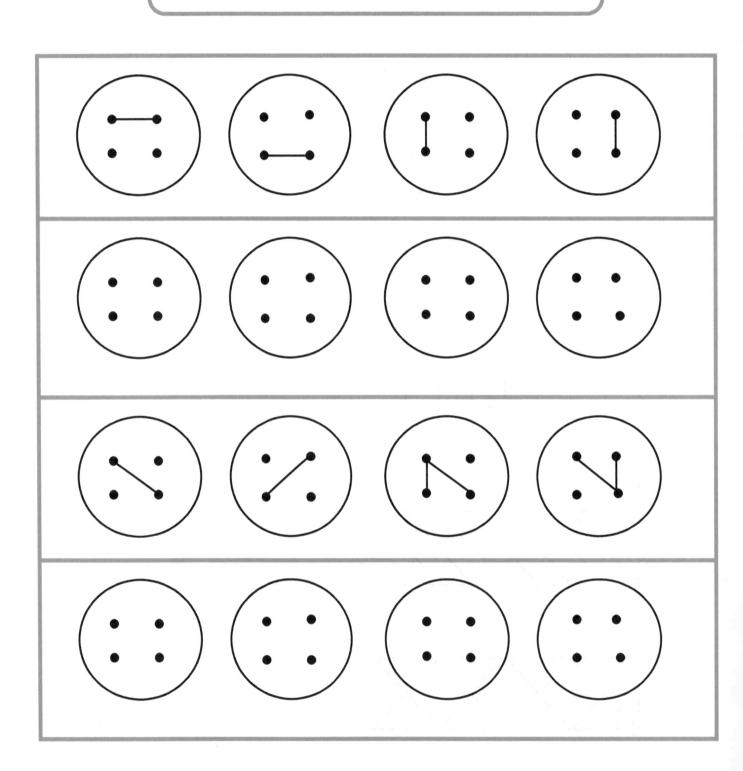

Copy the pattern from the top circle on the circle below it.

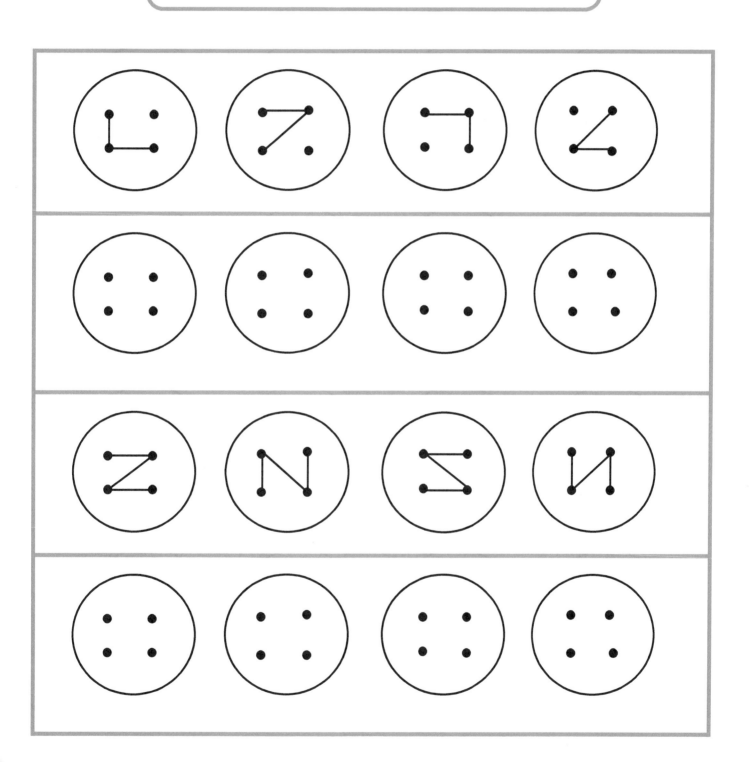

Copy the pattern from the top circle on the circle below it.

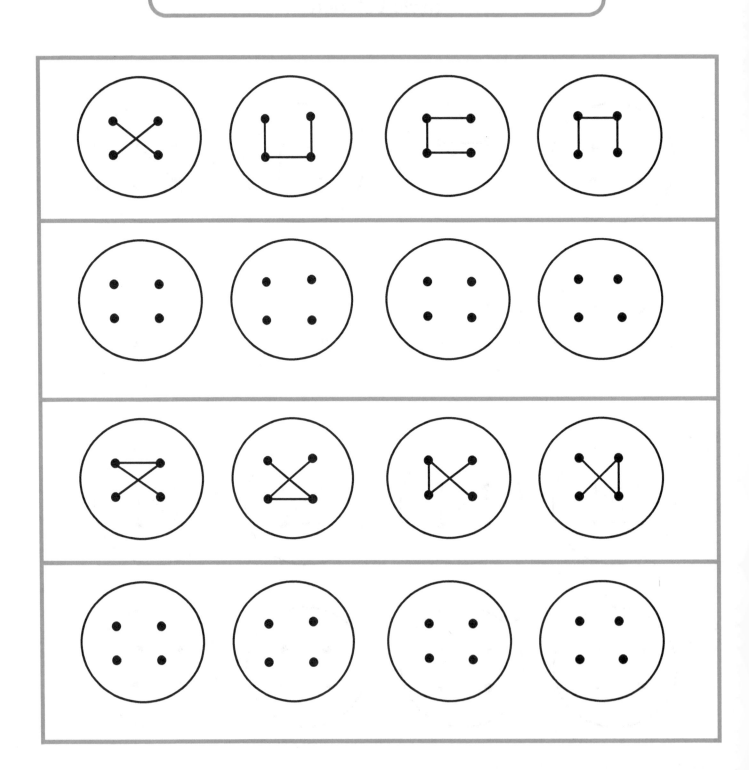

Copy the pattern from the top circle on the
circle below it.

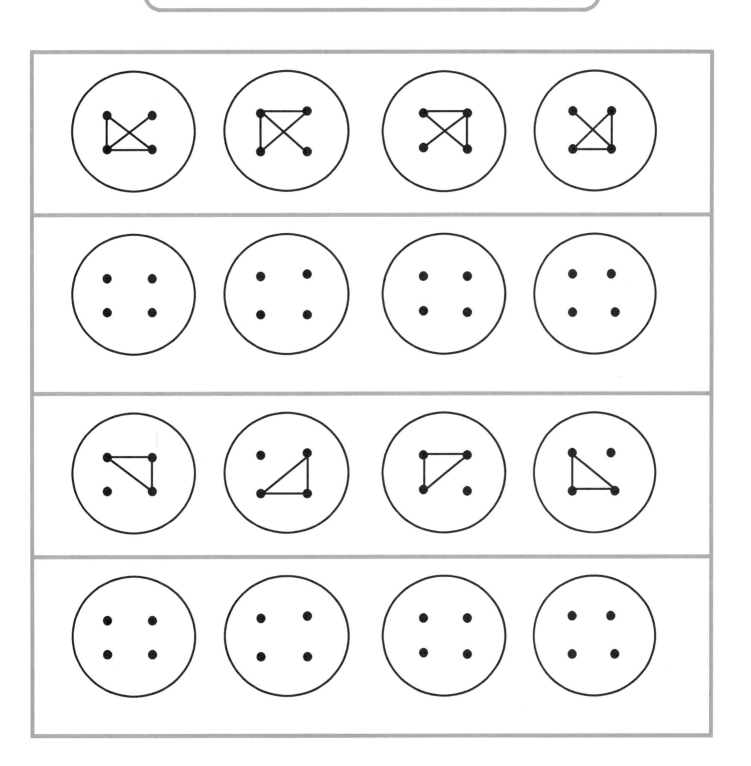

Copy the pattern from the top circle on the circle below it.

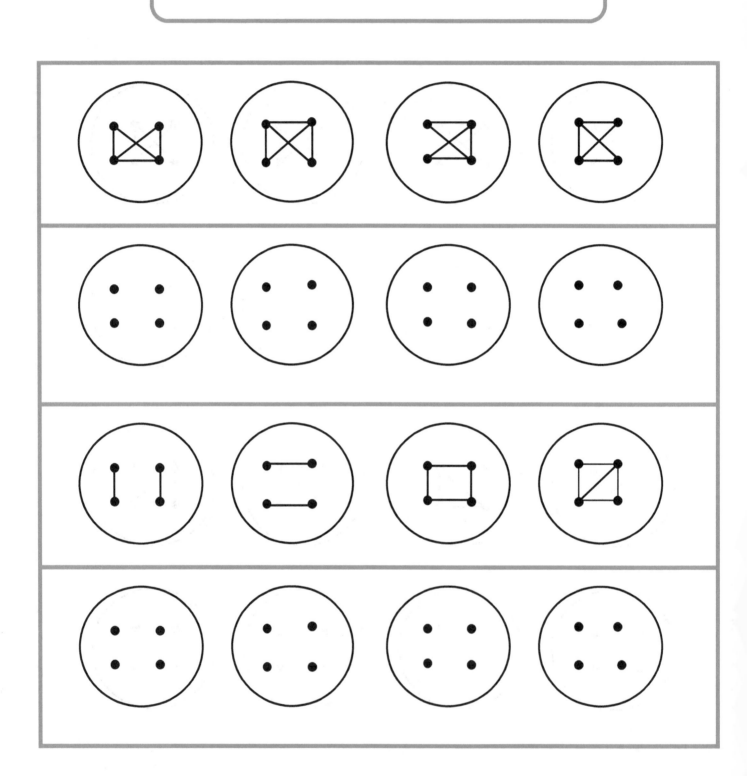

Color the dice that has the same number of dots as the first dice.

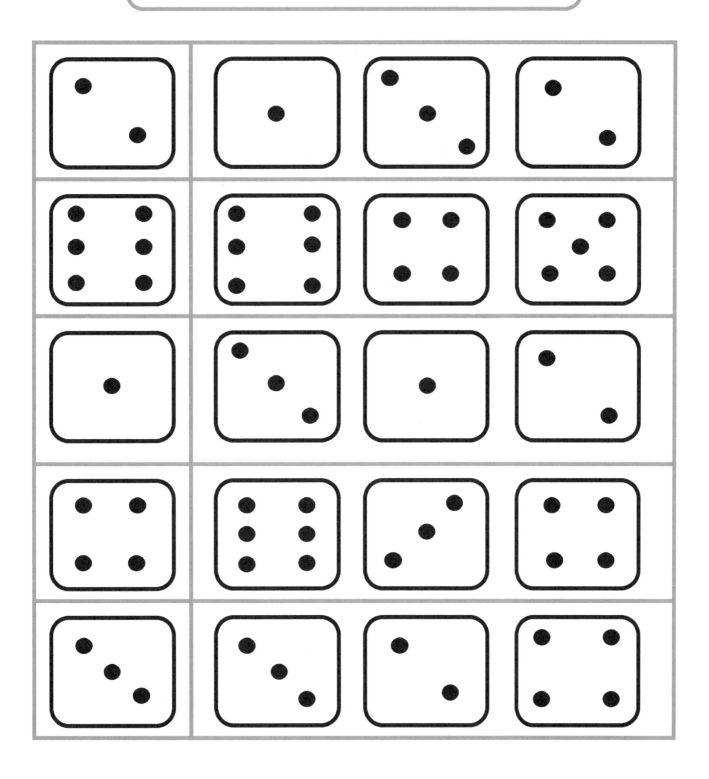

Color the dice that has the same number of dots as the first dice.

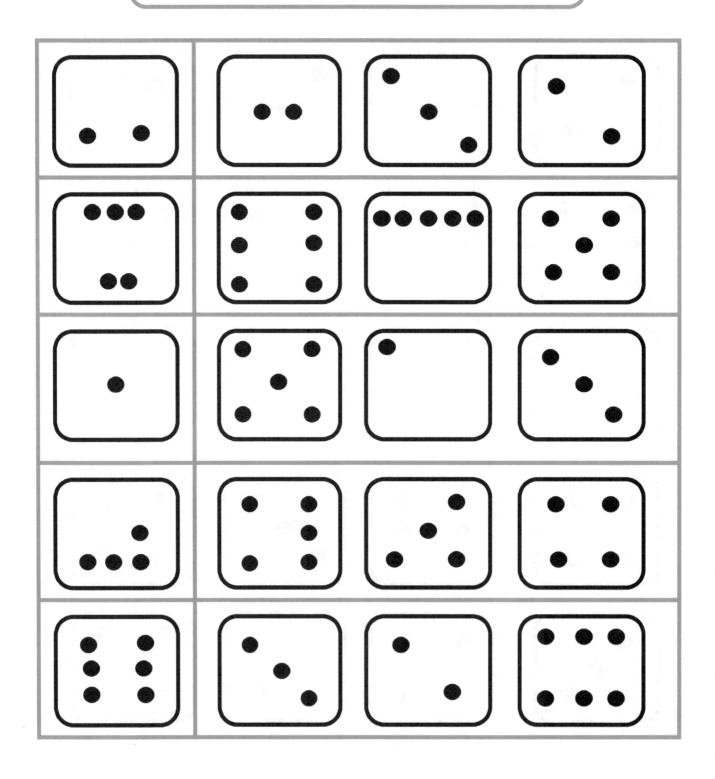

Color the dice that has the same number of dots as the first dice.

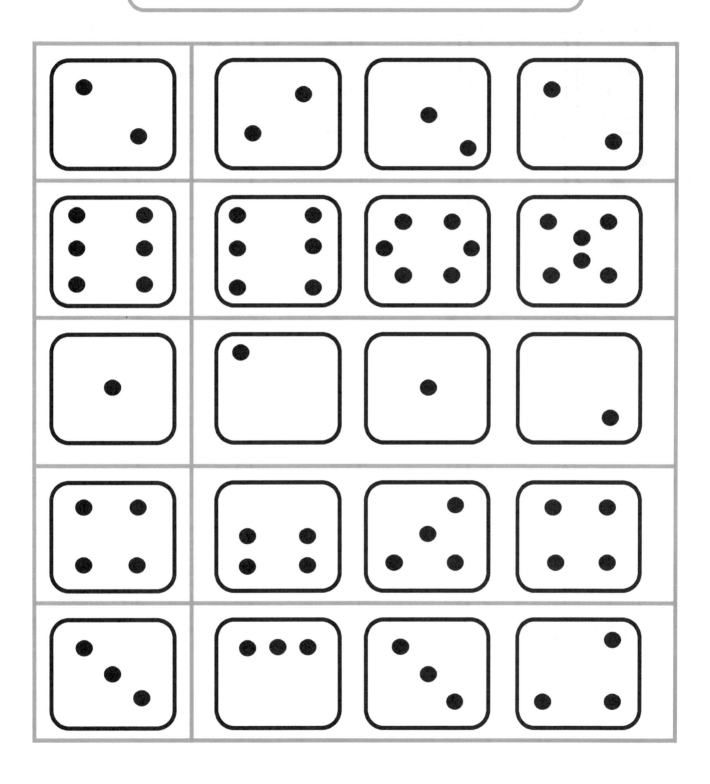

Continue the series.

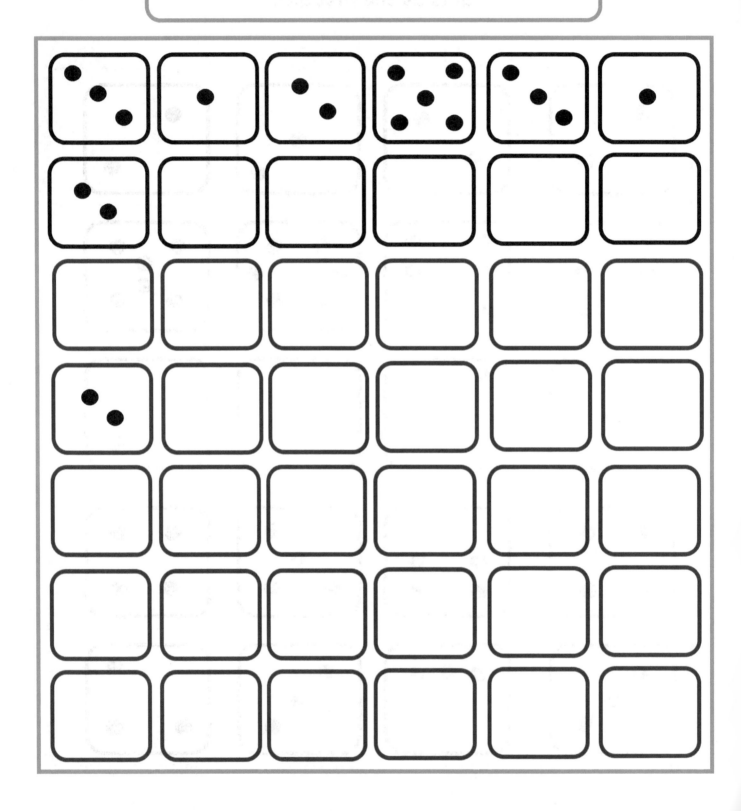

Continue the series.

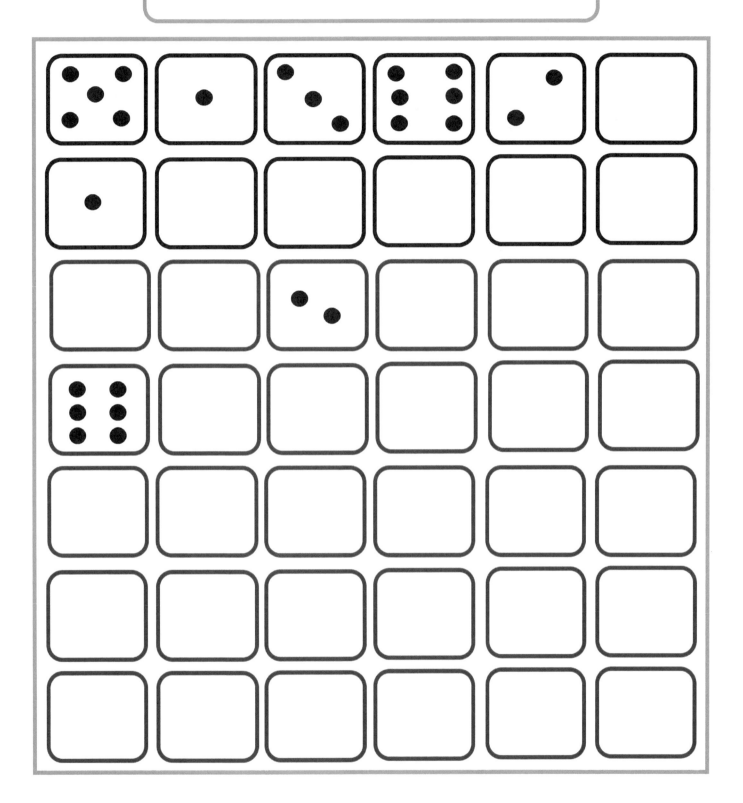

Continue the series.

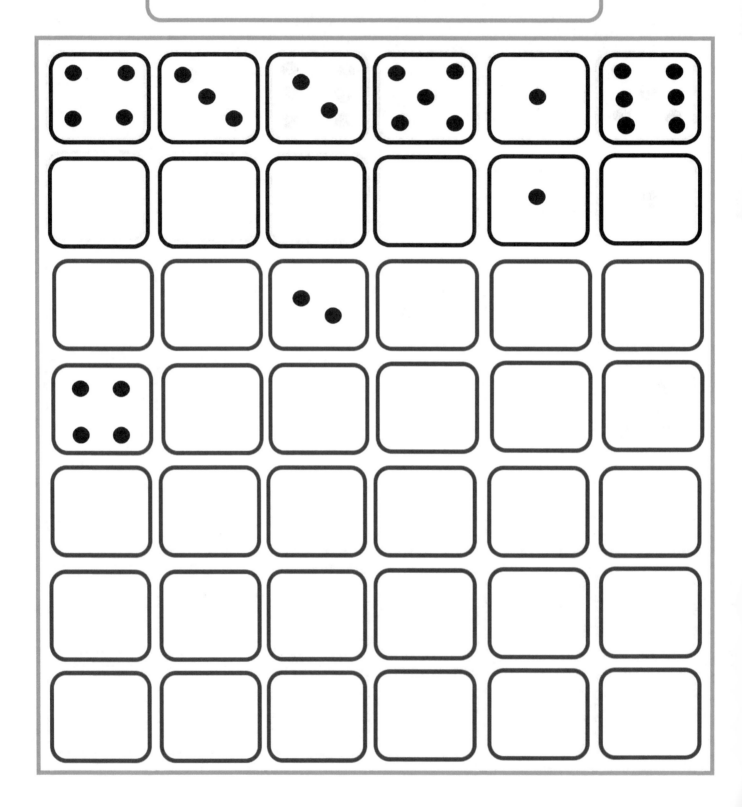

Continue the series.

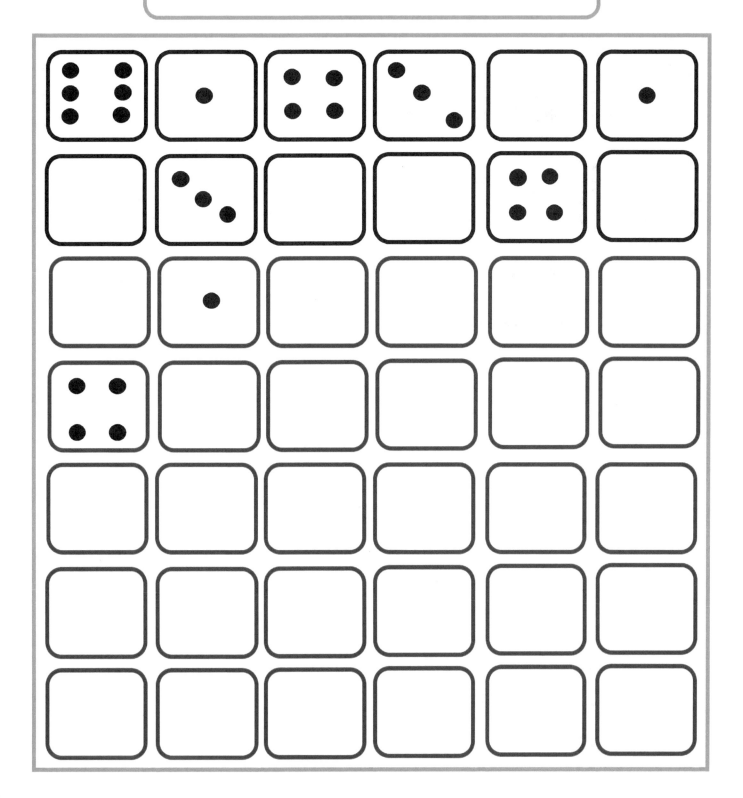

Continue the series.

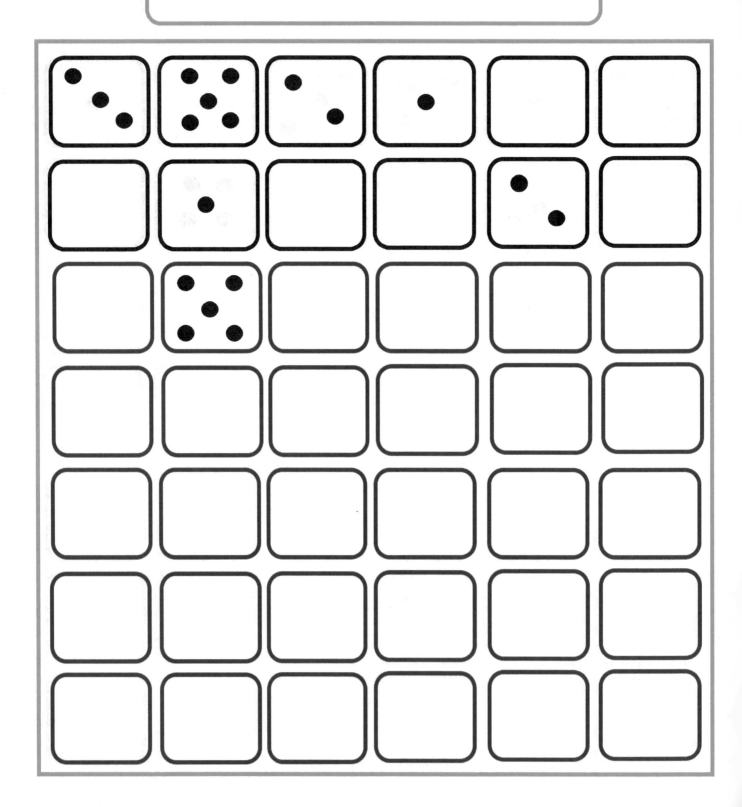

Color the same number of blocks as the
number of dots on the dice.

Color the same number of blocks as the number of dots on the dice.

Draw the picture that comes next in the pattern.

Draw the picture that comes next in the pattern.

Cut and paste the picture that comes next in the pattern.

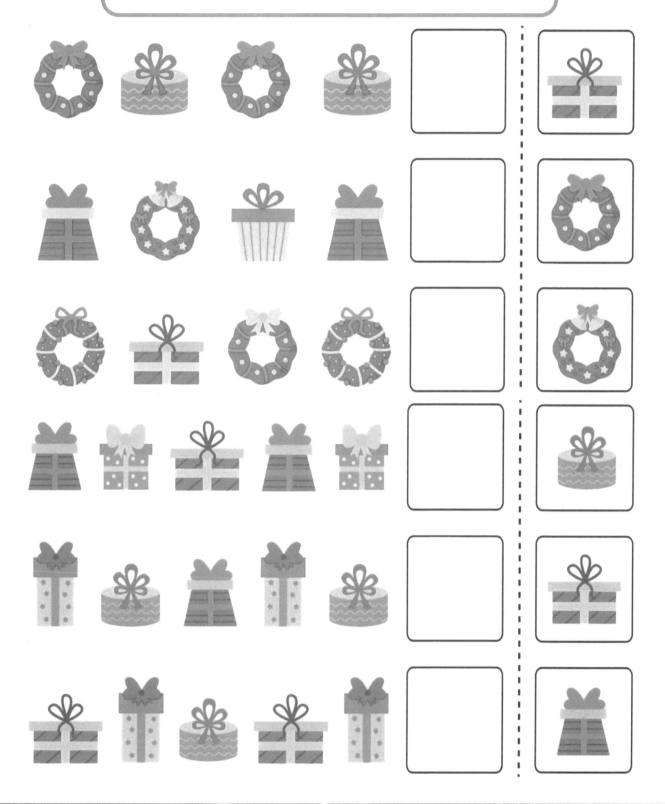

Cut and paste the picture that comes next in the pattern.

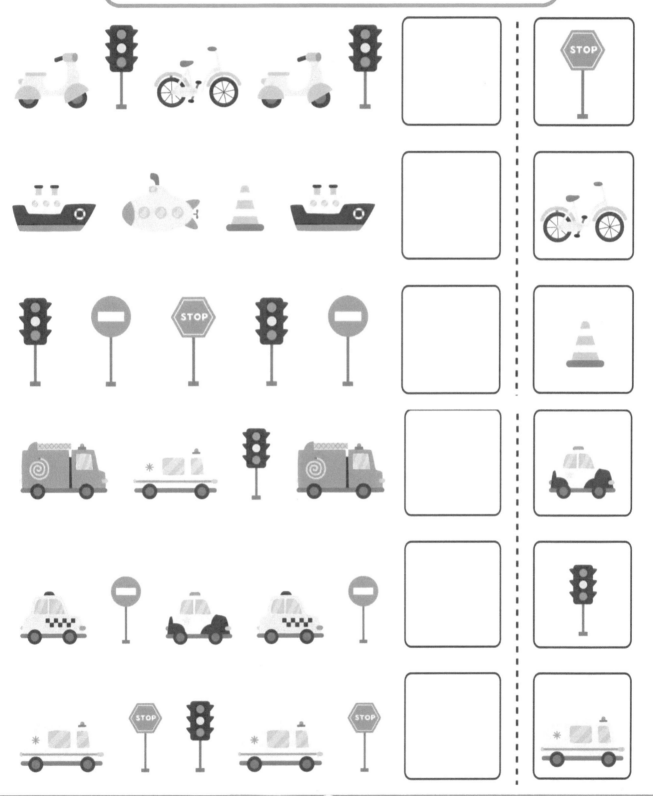

Cut and paste the picture that comes next in the pattern.

Match the halves.

Match the halves.

Match the halves.

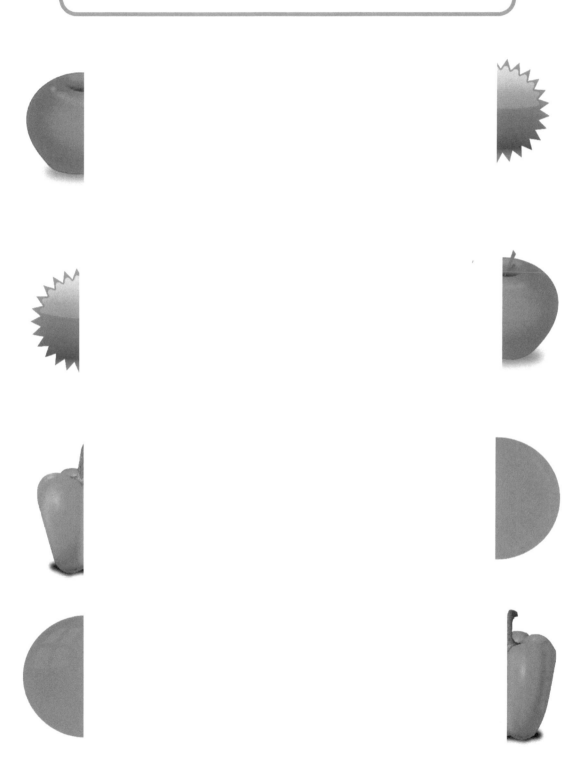

Match the halves.

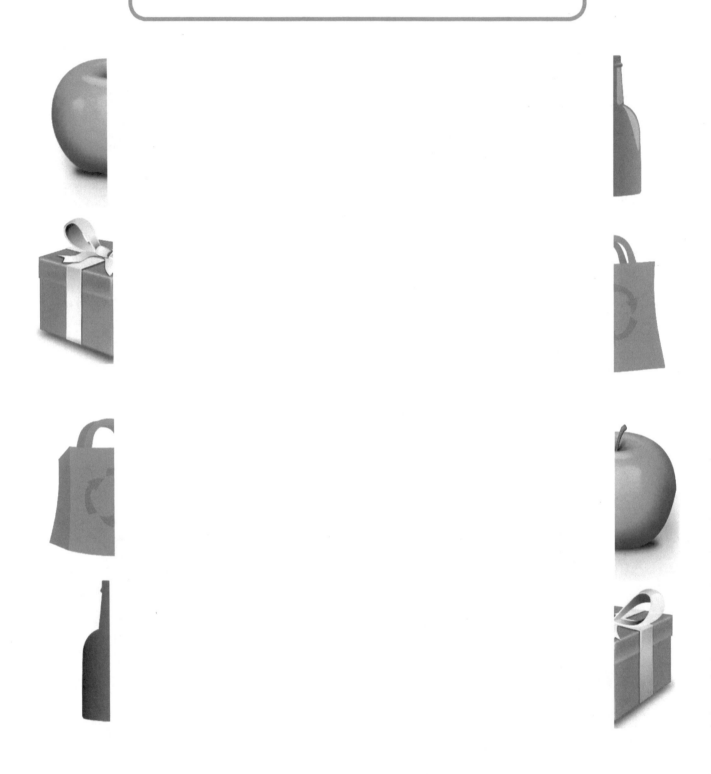

Trace and write.

Aa

alligator

A A A A A A

a a a a a a a

A A A A A A

a a a a a a a

The alligator is surfing in the sea.

The alligator is surfing in the sea.

The alligator is surfing in the sea.

Trace and write.

bird

B b

B B B B B

b b b b b b

B B B B B

b b b b b b

The bird is sitting in the nest.
The bird is sitting in the nest.
The bird is sitting in the nest.

Trace and write.

cat

C c

C C C C C

c c c c c c

C C C C C

c c c c c c

The cat is chasing the mouse.
The cat is chasing the mouse.
The cat is chasing the mouse.

Trace and write.

dog

Dd

D D D D D

d d d d d d

D D D D D

d d d d d d

The dog is playing in dirt.
The dog is playing in dirt.
The dog is playing in dirt.

Trace and write.

elephant

E e

E E E E E E E

e e e e e e e

E E E E E E E

e e e e e e e

An elephant is enjoying in the rain.
An elephant is enjoying in the rain.
An elephant is enjoying in the rain.

Trace and write.

fox

F f

E E E E E E

e e e e e e e

E E E E E E

e e e e e e e

The fox is trying to take the eggs.

The fox is trying to take the eggs.

The fox is trying to take the eggs.

Trace and write.

G g giraffe

G G G G G

g g g g g g g

G G G G G

g g g g g g g

The giraffe is driving the car.

The giraffe is driving the car.

The giraffe is driving the car.

Trace and write.

H h
horse

H H H H H H

h h h h h h

H H H H H

h h h h h h

The horse is jumping over the fence.
The horse is jumping over the fence.
The horse is jumping over the fence.

Trace and write.

insect

I i

i i i i i i i i i i

i i i i i i i i i

i i i i i i i i i

i i i i i i i i i

The insects are playing on a tree.

The insects are playing on a tree.

The insects are playing on a tree.

Trace and write.

jellyfish

jJ

J J J J J J

j j j j j j j

J J J J J J

j j j j j j j

The jellyfish is swimming in the water.
The jellyfish is swimming in the water.
The jellyfish is swimming in the water.

Trace and write.

koala

K k

K K K K K K

k k k k k k k

K K K K K K

k k k k k k k

The koala bear is playing on a tree trunk.

The koala bear is playing on a tree trunk.

The koala bear is playing on a tree trunk.

Trace and write.

L lion
Ll

L L L L L L L
l l l l l l l
L L L L L L L
l l l l l l l

The lion is jumping over the bushes.
The lion is jumping over the bushes.
The lion is jumping over the bushes.

Trace and write.

m
mouse M

M M M M

m m m m m

M M M M

m m m m m

The mouse is eating cheese.
The mouse is eating cheese.
The mouse is eating cheese.

Trace and write.

narwhal

N N N N N N

n n n n n n

N N N N N N

n n n n n n

The narwhal is swimming in the ocean.
The narwhal is swimming in the ocean.
The narwhal is swimming in the ocean.

Trace and write.

O o
owl

O O O O O

o o o o o o

O O O O O

o o o o o o

The owl is hooting from a tree.
The owl is hooting from a tree.
The owl is hooting from a tree.

Trace and write.

panda

P p

P P P P P P

p p p p p p

P P P P P P

p p p p p p

The panda is juggling fruit.
The panda is juggling fruit.
The panda is juggling fruit.

Trace and write.

Q quail
Qq

Q Q Q Q Q

q q q q q q q

Q Q Q Q Q

q q q q q q q

The quail is sitting in its nest.

The quail is sitting in its nest.

The quail is sitting in its nest.

Trace and write.

R r **rabbit**

R R R R R

r r r r r r r

R R R R R

r r r r r r r

The rabbit is hopping over the carrots.
The rabbit is hopping over the carrots.
The rabbit is hopping over the carrots.

Trace and write.

Ss

squirrel

S S S S S

s s s s s

s s s s s

s s s s s

The squirrel is sleeping.
The squirrel is sleeping.
The squirrel is sleeping.

Trace and write.

turtle

T
t T

T T T T T T

t t t t t t t

T T T T T T

t t t t t t t

The turtle is standing on a skateboard.
The turtle is standing on a skateboard.
The turtle is standing on a skateboard.

Trace and write.

unicorn

U u

U U U U U

u u u u u u u

U U U U U

u u u u u u u

The unicorn is playing on the clouds.
The unicorn is playing on the clouds.
The unicorn is playing on the clouds.

Trace and write.

vampire bat vV

V V V V V V

V V V V V V V

V V V V V V V

V V V V V V V

The vampire bat is taking all the candies.
The vampire bat is taking all the candies.
The vampire bat is taking all the candies.

Trace and write.

whale

W w

W W W W

w w w w w w

W W W W

w w w w w w

The whale is swimming in the ocean.
The whale is swimming in the ocean.
The whale is swimming in the ocean.

Trace and write.

X x x-ray

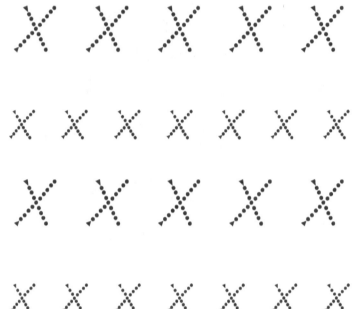

The ghost is having an x-ray.

The ghost is having an x-ray.

The ghost is having an x-ray.

Trace and write.

Yy
yak

Y Y Y Y Y Y Y

y y y y y y y y

Y Y Y Y Y Y Y

y y y y y y y y

The yak is sailing a boat.
The yak is sailing a boat.
The yak is sailing a boat.

Trace and write.

Zoo
Zz

Z Z Z Z Z

Z Z Z Z Z Z Z

Z Z Z Z Z Z

Z Z Z Z Z Z Z

The animals live in the zoo.
The animals live in the zoo.
The animals live in the zoo.

Trace and write.

The quick brown fox jumped over
the lazy dog.

Trace and write.

The quick brown fox jumped over the
lazy dog.

Trace and write.

The quick brown fox jumped over the lazy dog.

Trace and write.

The quick brown fox jumped over the lazy dog.

Trace and write.

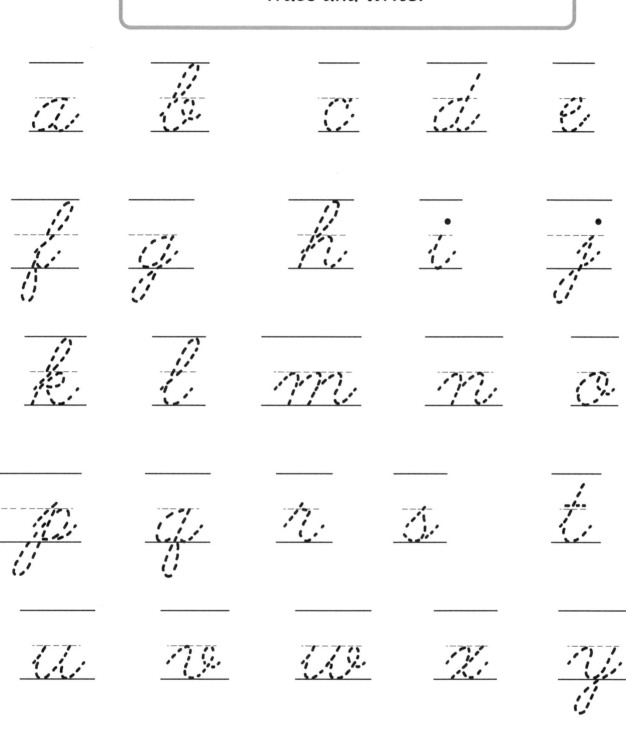

a   b   c   d   e

f   g   h   i   j

k   l   m   n   o

p   q   r   s   t

u   v   w   x   y

z

Trace and write.

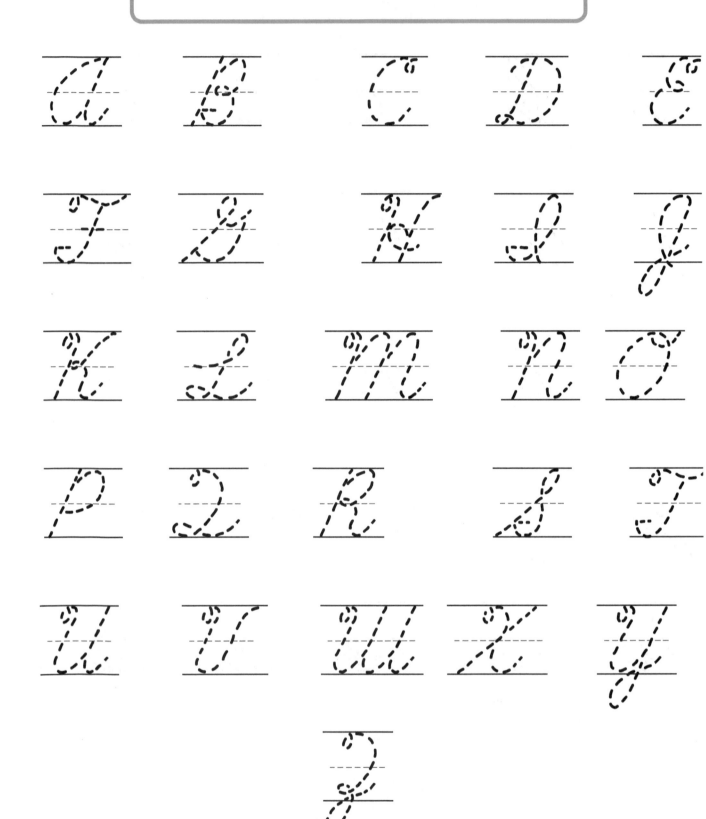

Trace and write.

The quick brown fox jumped over the lazy dog.

Made in United States
Troutdale, OR
10/27/2024

24181836R00060